CONTENTS

WELCOME TO THE WORLD OF INFOGRAPHICS

Using icons, graphics and pictograms, infographics visualise data and information in a whole new way!

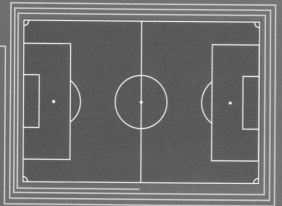

WRAP THE WORLD'S LONGEST COMIC STRIP AROUND A FOOTBALL PITCH

DISCOVER HOW MANY LEGO BRICKS IT TAKES TO CONNECT THE EARTH AND THE MOON

PLACE SOME OF THE WORLD'S LARGEST STATUES SIDE-BY-SIDE

LOOK AT THE WORLD'S BIGGEST VIOLIN NEXT TO AN ADULT HUMAN

Thousands of movies are released every year, thrilling people with stories of excitement, love and adventure. The most successful films can earn more than a billion dollars.

16 WEEKS

ET: The Extra-Terrestrial (1982)

15 WEEKS

Titanic (1997)

14 WEEKS

Tootsie (1982)
Beverly Hills Cop (1984)

MOST VEHICLES DESTROYED IN A FILM
TRANSFORMERS: DARK OF THE MOON (2011)

532

CHARACTERS WHO HAVE APPEARED IN THE MOST MOVIES

THE DEVIL
544 MOVIES

SANTA CLAUS
303 MOVIES

THE GRIM REAPER
290 MOVIES

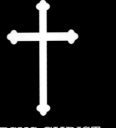

JESUS CHRIST
239 MOVIES

GOD
231 MOVIES

HIGHEST-GROSSING FILMS

These movies smashed all records by taking the most money at cinemas around the world.

AVATAR (2009)
US$ 2.8 BILLION

TITANIC (1997)
US$ 2.2 BILLION

GODZILLA
28 MOVIES

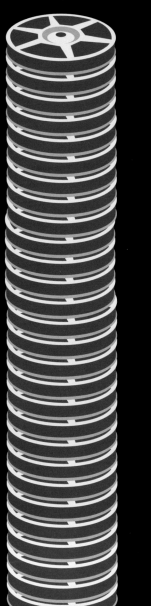

JAMES BOND
25 MOVIES

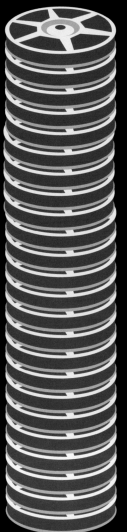

STAR TREK
FRIDAY THE 13TH
NATIONAL LAMPOON
12 MOVIES

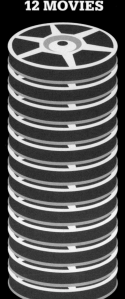

BATMAN
PINK PANTHER
11 MOVIES

MARVEL'S THE AVENGERS (2012)
US$ 1.5 BILLION

HARRY POTTER AND THE DEATHLY HALLOWS PART 2 (2011)
US$1.3 BILLION

TRANSFORMERS: DARK OF THE MOON (2011)
US$1.1 BILLION

Made for a budget of just US$15,000, horror movie *Paranormal Activity* took US$197 million at the box office – a return of more than 650,000 per cent.

MOVIE STARS

Big movies need big stars. With films earning huge amounts of money, the biggest stars can earn US$20 million for every movie they make.

MR SPIELBERG

The highest-grossing director of all time is Steven Spielberg. As of 2012, his 30 movies had taken US$9.38 billion at the box office around the world.

First words spoken on film
The Jazz Singer **(1926)**
Wait a minute, wait a minute. You ain't heard nothin' yet!
spoken by Al Jolson.

HIGHEST-PAID ACTORS

This is what Hollywood's top stars were paid between
MAY 2011 AND MAY 2012

TOM CRUISE
US$75 MILLION

LEONARDO DICAPRIO
US$37 MILLION

ADAM SANDLER
US$37 MILLION

DWAYNE JOHNSON
US$36 MILLION

HIGHEST-GROSSING MOVIE STARS

$$$$$$$$$$$$$$$$$$$$$$$$$$$$$$$$$$$$$$

FRANK WELKER (97 MOVIES) US$6.45 BILLION

$$$$$$$$$$$$$$$$$$$$$$$$$$$$$

SAMUEL L JACKSON (84 MOVIES) US$5.15 BILLION

$$$$$$$$$$$$$$$$$$$$$

TOM HANKS (44 MOVIES) US$4.24 BILLION

$$$$$$$$$$$$$$$$$$$

JOHN RATZENBERGER (32 MOVIES) US$3.91 BILLION

$$$$$$$$$$$$$$$$$$

EDDIE MURPHY (38 MOVIES) US$3.81 BILLION

FRANK WELKER

Frank Welker doesn't actually appear in his movies. Instead, he supplies voices for some of the most successful movies ever, including the Transformers series of films.

RIN TIN TIN

LASSIE

STRONGHEART

ANIMAL MOVIE STARS

Three dogs have stars on the Hollywood Walk of Fame. German Shepherd Rin Tin Tin starred in 20 films, while Strongheart was a movie star during the 1920s. Lassie is a character that has been portrayed on film and TV for more than 70 years and is in its 10th generation of dog actor.

KRISTEN STEWART
US$34.5 MILLION

CAMERON DIAZ
US$34 MILLION

BEN STILLER
US$33 MILLION

Rin Tin Tin used to sign his movie contracts using his paw print.

TELEVISION

The first television broadcasts began more than 80 years ago in 1936. Today, billions of people around the world tune in every day to watch variety shows, cookery programmes and soap operas.

LONG-RUNNING TV SHOWS

Sábado Gigante
variety show, **Chile**

1962 — over **2,000** episodes → **present**

1960 — *Hasta La Cocina*, cookery show, **Mexico**

1956 — *Guiding Light*, soap opera, **USA**

PANASONIC PRODUCE A
152-INCH
3-D HD-TV
WHICH MEASURES
3.4 M WIDE AND 1.8 M HIGH.

THE SMALLEST TV SCREEN, BUILT BY MICROEMISSIVE, MEASURES JUST
3.84 x 2.88 MM
WITH A RESOLUTION OF 160 X 120 PIXELS – IT'S SMALLER THAN YOUR FINGERNAIL.

■ ←···· ACTUAL SIZE

THE BIGGEST GAME SHOW WINNINGS
€3 MILLION
won by Nino Stefan on German Pro 7 show *Beat the Raab* in 2009.

The world's first TV advert appeared on **1 JULY 1941** for the Bulova Watch Company. The company paid **US$9.**

February 2012

Mon	Tue	Wed	Thu	Fri	Sat	Sun
30	31	1	2	3	4	5
6	7	8	9	10	11	12
13	14	15	16	17	18	19
20	21	22	23	24	25	26
27	28	29	1	2	3	4

Jeremiah Franco and Carin Shreve set the record for TV watching when they completed **86 hours 37 minutes** watching back-to-back *Simpsons* episodes from 8–12 February 2012.

more than **11,500** episodes → **present**

over **15,000** episodes **2009**

MOST EXPENSIVE TV SERIES

WHERE THE MONEY GOES

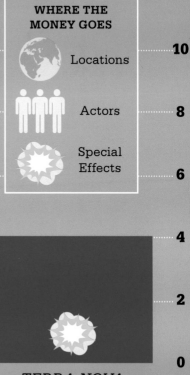

Locations

Actors

Special Effects

MILLION US$ PER EPISODE

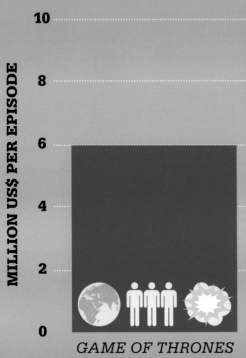

GAME OF THRONES (SEASON 1, 2011)

FRIENDS (FINAL SERIES, 2003)

TERRA NOVA (SEASON 1, 2011)

THE STAGE

Plays have been performed for more than 2,500 years and are still one of the most popular forms of entertainment. Every year, some 13 million people go to a theatre in the UK alone.

The world's oldest theatre was the **THEATRE OF DIONYSIUS** in Athens. Built around 500 BCE, it could seat **17,000** people.

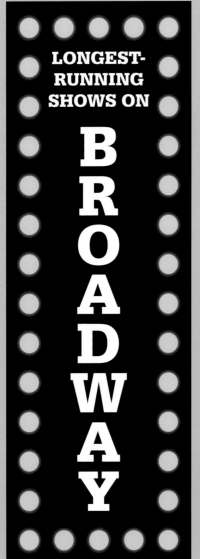

LONGEST-RUNNING SHOWS ON **BROADWAY**

PHANTOM OF THE OPERA **10,399** SHOWS

CATS **7,485** SHOWS

CHICAGO **6,725** SHOWS

LES MISÉRABLES **6,680** SHOWS

THE LION KING **6,325** SHOWS

as of January 2013

Actors should never whistle on stage. This belief dates back to old theatre riggers who used to communicate using whistles and could get confused.

SHORTEST AND LONGEST

The shortest play is *Breath* by Samuel Beckett. It is **35 seconds** long and has no actors – just sound effects and lighting changes. In contrast, *The Warp* by Neil Oram last for a total of **22 hours**. It is actually 10 individual shorter plays that are usually performed in one stage marathon.

35 seconds

The **biggest** theatre in the world today is the **Great Auditorium**, part of the Great Hall of the People in Tiananmen Square, **Beijing**, China. It can seat **10,000 people.**

THE WORLD'S **LONGEST RUNNING PLAY** IS *THE MOUSETRAP* by Dame Agatha Christie.

60 YEARS

SHAKESPEARE FACTS

He was responsible for 1,700 words we use every day, including *aerial, submerge, reliance, exposure, assassination* as well as several common phrases, including *break the ice it's all Greek to me one fell swoop*

HE WROTE AT LEAST

37 PLAYS

ONE OF WHICH, *CARDENIO,* IS LOST. THE FIRST, *LOVE'S LABOUR'S LOST,* WAS WRITTEN IN 1588–97 AND THE LAST, *HENRY VIII,* WAS WRITTEN IN 1613.

It is considered bad luck to wish someone "good luck" in a theatre. Instead, actors may wish each other to **"BREAK A LEG".**

THEATRE SUPERSTITIONS

Actors believe you should never refer to Shakespeare's play *Macbeth* by its name. Instead, they call it **"THE SCOTTISH PLAY".**

AWARDS

Outstanding achievements in film and TV are often recognised with awards at glamorous ceremonies. Categories include acting and directing, as well as costume design and special effects. There are also awards for some of the worst shows and performances.

THE ACADEMY AWARDS

Academy Awards, or Oscars, are awarded for special achievements in movies. Categories include best actor and actress and best film.

4

Katharine Hepburn has won more Oscars than any other actor or actress. She has won four best actress Oscars.

Three films hold the record for the most Oscar wins with 11 – *Ben Hur* (1959), *Titanic* (1997) and *The Return of the King* (2003).

11

THE RETURN OF THE KING IS THE ONLY MOVIE TO WIN ALL THE OSCARS IT WAS NOMINATED FOR.

22

Walt Disney has personally won more Oscars than anyone else. He was nominated 59 times and won 22.

AN **OSCAR** WEIGHS JUST OVER **3 KG** AND IS **34 CM** TALL.

THE BAFTA AWARDS

The British Academy of Film and Television Arts gives awards for TV and movies.

Film director **Woody Allen** has won eight awards for his movies, such as *Annie Hall*.

THE OLIVIER AWARDS

The Laurence Olivier Awards are presented for achievements in British theatre.

The musical *Matilda* holds the record for the most awards in one year, winning seven in 2012.

THE EMMY AWARDS

Awarded for achievements on US television

AN **EMMY** WEIGHS JUST OVER **3 KG** AND IS **39 CM** TALL.

8

Most Emmys won by a female performer: **Cloris Leachman**.

7

Most Emmys won by a male performer: **Edward Asner**.

Most Emmys won by a series: *Frasier*.

37

THE RAZZIES

The Golden Raspberry, or Razzie, is awarded to bad films and performances.

Adam Sandler holds the record for winning the most with **11 Razzies.**

BOOKS

Books come in all sizes, from the gigantic to the microscopic. Today, the development of e-books means that you can carry an entire library of books in the palm of your hand.

FIVE LONGEST NOVELS IN THE ENGLISH LANGUAGE

SIRONIA, TEXAS
MADISON COOPER
1952

POOR FELLOW MY COUNTRY
XAVIER HERBERT
1975

1.2 MILLION WORDS

1.1 MILLION WORDS

969,000 WORDS

850,000 WORDS

700,000 WORDS

MISSION EARTH
L. RON HUBBARD
1985

CLARISSA
SAMUEL RICHARDSON
1748

MISS MACINTOSH, MY DARLING
MARGUERITE YOUNG
1965

THE CODEX LEICESTER
Leonardo da Vinci
(c. 1510)
US$30.8 MILLION

MOST EXPENSIVE BOOK

The most expensive book ever sold, *The Codex Leicester*, is a 32-page document that was written in 1506–1510 by Leonardo da Vinci.

It was written in Leonardo's distinctive mirror writing

ВACKWARDS!

THE ST CUTHBERT GOSPEL
(c. 650)
US$14.1 MILLION

THE GOSPELS OF HENRY THE LION
Order of St Benedict
(c. 1175)
US$11.7 MILLION

BIRDS OF AMERICA
James Audubon
(c. 1830)
US$11.5 MILLION

THE CANTERBURY TALES Geoffrey
Chaucer (c. 1400)
US$7.5 MILLION

Made in 2007, the world's smallest book measures just **0.07 x 0.1 mm** – smaller than the full stop at the end of this sentence. It is *Teeny Ted from Turnip Town* and each page was carved onto silicon using a laser. It can only be read using a powerful microscope.

THE BIGGEST LIBRARY IN THE WORLD

LIBRARY OF CONGRESS
WASHINGTON D.C., USA

151.8 MILLION ITEMS, INCLUDING **34.5 MILLION BOOKS** AND OTHER PRINTED MATERIALS IN **470 LANGUAGES**

EMPLOYS **3,525** PERMANENT MEMBERS OF STAFF

1,380 KM OF BOOKSHELVES

1.7 MILLION VISITORS EVERY YEAR

1,004,725

approximate number of books published around the world each year

ONE OF THE WORLD'S LARGEST BOOKS IS THE KLENCKE ATLAS, WHICH MEASURES 1.75 X 1.9 M. IT IS 350 YEARS OLD...

... AND TAKES SIX PEOPLE TO LIFT IT.

RISE OF THE E-BOOK
US e-book sales

US$2.1 MILLION	US$25.2 MILLION	US$441.3 MILLION	US$621.3 MILLION
2002	2006	2010	2012

COMICS

Since the first comic book was published in 1837, cartoon strips have created invincible super-heroes and action-packed adventures that have even made it onto the big screen.

Comic timeline

First appearance of super-heroes

First appearance of comic strips

WONDER WOMAN
All Star Comics #8

CAPTAIN AMERICA
Captain America Comics #1

1941

SUPERMAN
Action Comics #1

1938

BRENDA STARR

1940

BLONDIE

1930

1897

1918

GASOLINE ALLEY

1924

ANNIE

1930

DICK TRACY

1937

PRINCE VALIANT

1939

BATMAN
Detective Comics #27

THE KATZENJAMMER KIDS

THE LARGEST GRAPHIC NOVEL
Romeo and Juliet: The War by Stan Lee. A limited collector's edition measured

FIRST COMIC SUPERHERO
THE PHANTOM, CREATED BY LEE FALK IN 1936

63.18 cm   83.83 cm

Just 25 copies were printed.

COMIC BOOK CONVENTIONS
Comic-Con in the USA attracts some **125,000**. The busiest comic festival is Japan's **Comiket**. In 2012 **560,000** visited the festival.

THE LONGEST COMIC STRIP

Drawn by French students in 2011, the longest comic strip measured more than 1,000 m long – enough to wrap around a football pitch more than three times.

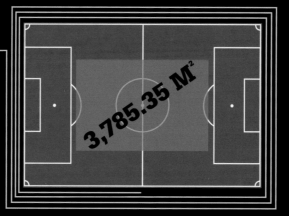

3,785.35 M²

THE LARGEST COMIC STRIP

Drawn in Japan in 2010 and made up of 13 panels, with each panel showing a player from the Japanese football team. It measured 3,785.35 m² – more than half a football pitch.

DENNIS THE MENACE

1951

1963

THE AVENGERS
The Avengers #1

FIRST GRAPHIC NOVEL
BLOODSTAR BY RICHARD CORBEN (1976)

1950

1958

1962

BEETLE BAILEY

B.C.

SPIDERMAN
Amazing Fantasy #15

In 2010, a copy of the 1938 comic in which Superman first appeared *ACTION COMICS #1* sold for **US$2.16 MILLION**

The original cover price was **10 cents**.

To buy it in 2010, you would have needed a stack of 10 cent coins 29 km tall – more than three times the height of Everest.

10c

1938

2010

Since it was first printed in 1950, the comic strip *Peanuts* has appeared in more than **2,500** newspapers around the world, and read by some **355,000,000** people.

MUSIC

Musical pieces can be long operas or even short periods of silence, while the groups that play them can contain thousands of instrument players and singers.

4'33" BY JOHN CAGE

The piece involves a pianist sitting at a piano for four minutes and 33 seconds without playing a single note.

1,000 YEARS

The length of time it would take to perform *The Longplayer* by Jem Finer. The piece is being played out by computers at listening posts in the UK, USA, Egypt and Australia and will not finish until the year 2999.

LONG OPERAS

THE HERETICS
GABRIEL VON WAYDITCH
8 HOURS 30 MINUTES

THE LIFE AND TIMES OF JOSEPH STALIN
ROBERT WILSON
13 HOURS 25 MINUTES

LARGEST CHOIR

121,440

singers assembled in January 2011 at Perugalathur, India.

THE WORLD'S LARGEST VIOLIN

Built by 15 skilled workers, the world's largest violin is

4.27 M LONG

and takes three musicians to play.

MOST EXPENSIVE MUSICAL INSTRUMENT

A Stradivarius violin, called the Lady Blunt, was sold for

US$15.9 MILLION

in 2011 to raise money for the Japanese Tsunami Relief Fund.

ORCHESTRA

How the instruments in an orchestra are arranged.

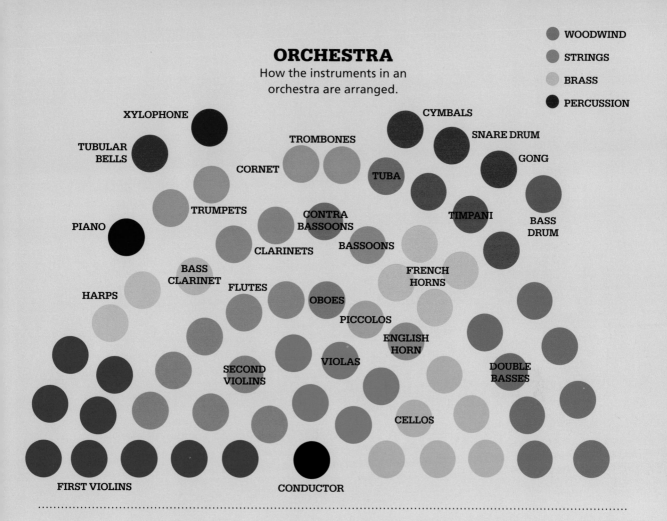

WOODWIND
STRINGS
BRASS
PERCUSSION

XYLOPHONE
TUBULAR BELLS
CORNET
TROMBONES
CYMBALS
SNARE DRUM
GONG
TUBA
TRUMPETS
CONTRA BASSOONS
TIMPANI
BASS DRUM
PIANO
CLARINETS
BASSOONS
BASS CLARINET
FRENCH HORNS
HARPS
FLUTES
OBOES
PICCOLOS
ENGLISH HORN
SECOND VIOLINS
VIOLAS
DOUBLE BASSES
FIRST VIOLINS
CONDUCTOR
CELLOS

In 1998, nearly

4,000

children formed an enormous orchestra to play Sir Malcolm Arnold's *Little Suite No 2*. The orchestra included **1,600 string players**, **1,300 woodwind**, **800 brass** and more than **200 percussion**.

MUSICAL SYMBOLS

Musicians use various symbols to show the notes of a piece of music. This is called musical notation.

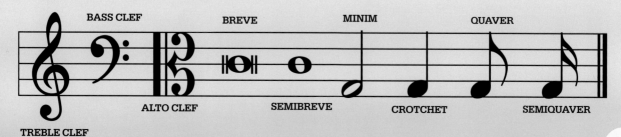

BASS CLEF
BREVE
MINIM
QUAVER
ALTO CLEF
SEMIBREVE
CROTCHET
SEMIQUAVER
TREBLE CLEF

19

ROCK AND POP

Sales of rock and pop music have earned performers millions of dollars and turned them into global superstars.

BIGGEST SELLING ALBUMS OF ALL TIME

THRILLER **(1982)**
MICHAEL JACKSON

65 MILLION

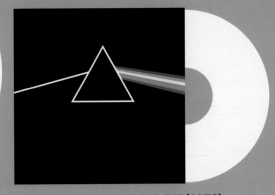

THE DARK SIDE OF THE MOON **(1973)**
PINK FLOYD

50 MILLION

THE GRAMMY AWARDS

The Grammys are awarded by the National Academy of Recording Arts and Sciences of the United States for achievements in the recording industry.

8 **Michael Jackson** (1984) and **Santana** (2000) hold the record for winning the most grammys in a single year, with eight.

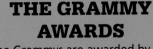

The best-selling single of all time

50,000,000

WHITE CHRISTMAS (1942)
BING CROSBY

Longest gig

Rock musician Bruce Springsteen played a concert on 31 July 2012 in Helsinki, Finland, that lasted four hours and six minutes, breaking his own record for the longest gig.

DIGITAL 50.5%

PHYSICAL 49.5%

DIGITAL VS PHYSICAL

In 2011, digital music sales in the US overtook physical sales (CDs and records) for the first time, making up 50.5% of all sales.

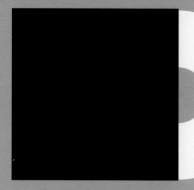

BACK IN BLACK **(1980)**
AC/DC

49 MILLION

THE BODYGUARD **(1992)**
WHITNEY HOUSTON/VARIOUS

44 MILLION

BAT OUT OF HELL **(1977)**
MEAT LOAF

43 MILLION

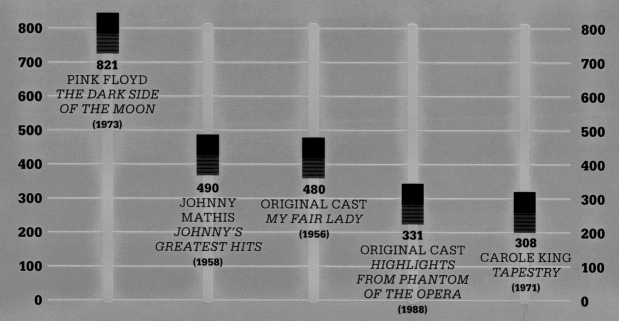

821
PINK FLOYD
*THE DARK SIDE
OF THE MOON*
(1973)

490
JOHNNY
MATHIS
*JOHNNY'S
GREATEST HITS*
(1958)

480
ORIGINAL CAST
MY FAIR LADY
(1956)

331
ORIGINAL CAST
*HIGHLIGHTS
FROM PHANTOM
OF THE OPERA*
(1988)

308
CAROLE KING
TAPESTRY
(1971)

MOST WEEKS IN THE US BILLBOARD CHARTS
(as of January 2013)

PLAYTIME

Toys and games aren't just for kids! Super-sized and super-expensive versions of classic play things have broken world records and become global sensations.

RUBIK'S CUBE

 The puzzle was invented in **1974** by Hungarian professor Ernö Rubik.

 More than **300 million** have been sold around the world.

 In June 2011, Feliks Zemdegs solved a cube in just **5.66 seconds.**

BIGGEST RUBIK'S CUBE WEIGHS MORE THAN
500 KG
OR SEVEN ADULT MALES

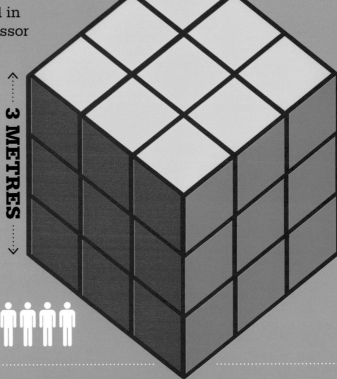

3 METRES

BIGGEST SKATEBOARD

The world's biggest skateboard weighs more than 1,600 kg and is
11.14 M LONG

Some of the **oldest toys** have been found in the remains of **ancient Sumer** and date back to **2600** BCE. They are simple figures of people and animals.

CHESS

Chess is one of the oldest board games in the world. It first appeared in India in the 6th century CE.

The world's most expensive chess set has pieces made of gold and platinum and studded with rubies, emeralds and diamonds. It's value is

US$9.8 MILLION

A TEDDY BEAR MADE BY GERMAN COMPANY STEIFF, SOLD FOR A RECORD

US$171,600 AT AUCTION IN 1994.

More than **275 million** Monopoly sets have been sold in **111** countries and **43** languages.

40 billion LEGO bricks stacked together would reach the Moon.

The number of LEGO bricks produced each year. That is 68,000 every single minute.

36 BILLION

GAMING

While the first video games were made up of simple dots and lines, today's gamers can play super-realistic games and compete with people on the other side of the world.

LARGEST WORKING GAMES CONTROLLER

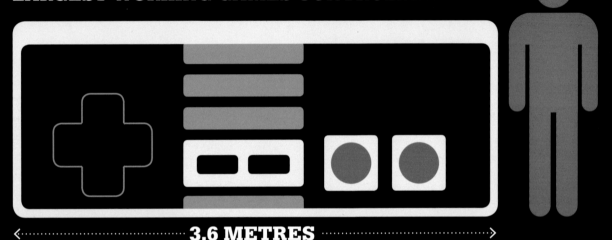

⟨········· **3.6 METRES** ·········⟩

A massive NES Games controller weighing 120 kg was built in 2012 by engineering students from TU Delft University, Netherlands.

CHRIS MCGIVERN FROM THE UK SPENT

**20 HOURS
24 MINUTES
43 SECONDS**

SETTING A DANCE GAME MARATHON RECORD IN 2011 PLAYING *DANCE DANCE REVOLUTION*.

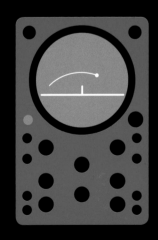

In 1958, William Higinbotham developed *Tennis for Two*. It was one of the first computer games and showed a simple tennis match on a round screen.

GROWTH OF THE VIDEO GAMES INDUSTRY

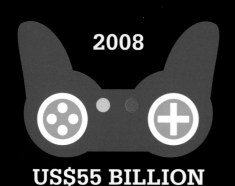

2008

US$55 BILLION

2012

US$68 BILLION

In comparison, the movie industry was only worth US$32 billion in 2012.

POPULAR GAMES CONSOLES (IN UNITS SOLD)

Nintendo DS 153 million

Wii 99 million

Xbox 76 million

PlayStation 70 million

SOCIAL GAMING

Social network game *CityVille* managed to collect 26 million online players within 12 days of its launch. That is more people than the population of Australia.

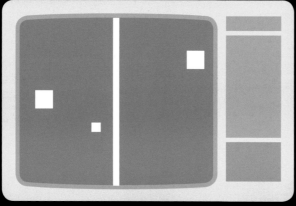

THE FIRST HOME VIDEO GAMES CONSOLE

Magnavox Odyssey launched in 1972 with simple line and dot games, such as *Pong*.

PAINTING AND PHOTOGRAPHY

Works of art can be created on any surface, including canvas, paper and glass. The best examples will sell for millions of dollars – even if they are painted onto the sides of buildings!

The world's most expensive photograph is *Rhine II* taken by Andreas Gursky from Germany. In 2011, it was sold for US$4.3 million.

PABLO PICASSO

is recognised as the most prolific painter ever. During his career of 75 years, he produced

 100,000
PRINTS AND ENGRAVINGS

 34,000
BOOK ILLUSTRATIONS

 13,500
PAINTINGS

 300
SCULPTURES AND CERAMICS

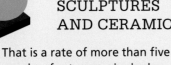 That is a rate of more than five works of art every single day.

The **frescoes** on the ceiling of the **Sistine Chapel** took Michelangelo **four years** to complete (1508–1512). The Chapel itself is 40.23 m long and 13.4 m wide.

MOST EXPENSIVE WORKS OF ART

US$250 MILLION

The Card Players, **1893**
Paul Cézanne

US$140 MILLION

No.5, 1948, **1948**
Jackson Pollock

US$137.5 MILLION

Woman III, **1953**
Willem de Kooning

US$135 MILLION

Portrait of Adele Bloch-Bauer, **1907**
Gustav Klimt

US$119.9 MILLION

The Scream, **1885**
Edvard Munch

LONGEST PAINTING MEASURES 6,000 M LONG AND WAS PAINTED BY 3,000 SCHOOL STUDENTS FROM MEXICO.

The Hermitage Museum
(St Petersburg, Russia), has more than

**2.7 MILLION EXHIBITS,
24 KM OF GALLERIES,
1,786 DOORS, 1,945 WINDOWS AND
1,057 HALLS AND ROOMS.**

In 1997, street artist Saber created an enormous piece of graffiti. Painted on the concrete banks of the Los Angeles River it needed more than 350 litres of paint and took the artist 35 nights to complete.

Perhaps the most famous painting in the World is the *Mona Lisa* (or *La Gioconda*) by **Leonardo da Vinci**. It hangs in the Musée du Louvre in Paris, France, and measures 77 x 53 cm.

SCULPTURE AND INSTALLATION

Some of the biggest art works of all, installations and statues can cover enormous areas and rise tens of metres into the sky.

Artists Christo and Jeanne-Claude are well-known for creating huge works of art. In 1991, they installed **3,100** umbrellas in long chains across valleys in Japan and the USA. The Japan chain measured **19 km long,** while the US chain measured **29 km long.**

Their *Surrounded Islands* project from 1983 saw them use **603,870 sq m of bright pink plastic** to wrap around the coasts of 11 islands in Biscayne Bay near Miami, Florida, USA.

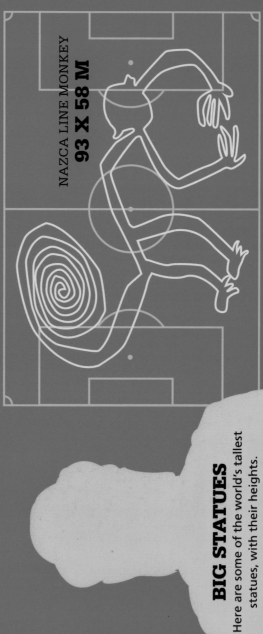

NAZCA LINE MONKEY
93 X 58 M

FOOTBALL PITCH 105 X 68 M

NAZCA LINES

These are huge line drawings made on the desert floor of Peru. They stretch over an area of 500 sq km and were made more than 2,000 years ago. They show plants and animals, and individual pictures are up to 235 m long.

BIG STATUES

Here are some of the world's tallest statues, with their heights.

SPRING TEMPLE BUDDHA
LUSHAN, HENAN, CHINA
128 M

LARGEST MODELLING BALLOON SCULPTURE

A spider measuring 6.76 m across and made from 2,975 balloons was installed in a waterpark in Grand Mound, Washington, USA in 2011.

THE MOTHERLAND CALLS
MAMAYEV, RUSSIA

85 M

In 1917, French artist Marcel Duchamp made art history when he took a urinal and turned it into a work of art by laying it on its back and calling it *Fountain*.

CHRIST THE REDEEMER
RIO DE JANEIRO, BRAZIL

39.6 M

STATUE OF LIBERTY
NEW YORK, USA

93 M

GLOSSARY

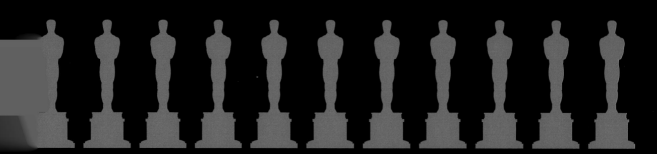

atlas
A collection of maps in a book.

broadcast
The transmission of a TV or radio programme to the public.

ceramics
Objects made from soft clay, which are then heated to a high temperature in order to make them hard.

comic strip
A short story told in a series of cartoon pictures, often printed in newspapers.

director
The person in charge of making a movie, who tells the actors and crew what they have to do.

console
A special type of computer used for playing video games.

e-book
A book that is read on an electronic device known as an e-reader.

folio
A book made of sheets of paper that have been folded in the middle.

HD-TV
High-definition television – a type of TV that shows images in great detail.

highest grossing
Something that has made the most amount of money. Gross is the total amount of money earned by selling something before deductions (the amount of money spent on making the item). The total gross minus the deductions is the profit.

library
A collection of reading and artistic materials, such as books, newspapers and records. Libraries can often be visited by people who want to study or borrow the materials.

novel

A fictional story mostly printed in book form. Graphic novels tell stories using pictures and words.

opera

A drama where the actors sing to music played by an orchestra. An opera is also a building where theatrical performances are staged.

orchestra

A large group of musicians who play various instruments including strings, woodwinds, brass and percussion.

prolific

Producing a lot of work – a prolific author has written a lot of books.

return

The amount of money made by selling something.

silicon

A material on which tiny marks can be made using a laser. These marks can hold a lot of information, which is why silicon is used to make computers and other electronic devices.

soap opera

A long-running TV series featuring one set of characters.

superstition

A belief that doing something will somehow affect something else, even if the two things seem unrelated.

Walk of Fame

A pavement in Hollywood, USA, where the names of famous movie stars have been engraved in stars.

Websites

MORE INFO:
www.movingimage.us
The website of the Museum of the Moving Image which is dedicated to the history of film and TV. It has teaching resources and online activities.

www.lovereading4kids.co.uk
An online bookstore and book review site offering recommendations for all ages and advice for parents.

www.classicsforkids.com
An online children's guide to classical music with tunes to listen to, musical tutorials and games.

MORE GRAPHICS:
www.visualinformation.info
A website that contains a whole host of infographic material on subjects as diverse as natural history, science, sport and computer games.

www.coolinfographics.com
A collection of infographics and data visualisations from other online resources, magazines and newspapers.

www.dailyinfographic.com
A comprehensive collection of infographics on an enormous range of topics that is updated every single day!

INDEX

ACKNOWLEDGEMENTS

First published in 2013 by Wayland

Copyright © Wayland 2013

Wayland
338 Euston Road
London NW1 3BH

Wayland Australia
Level 17/207 Kent Street
Sydney NSW 2000

All rights reserved.
Senior editor: Julia Adams

Produced by Tall Tree Ltd
Editors: Jon Richards and Joe Fullman
Designer: Ed Simkins
Consultant: Clive Gifford

Dewey classification: 700

ISBN: 9780750279628

Printed in China
Wayland is a division of Hachette
Children's Books, an Hachette UK company.
www.hachette.co.uk

The website addresses (URLs) included in this
book were valid at the time of going to press.
However, because of the nature of the Internet,
it is possible that some addresses may have
changed, or sites may have changed or closed
down, since publication. While the author and
Publisher regret any inconvenience this may
cause the readers, no responsibility for any such
changes can be accepted by either the author
or the Publisher.

GET THE PICTURE!

Welcome to the world of **infographics!** Icons, pictograms and graphics create an exciting form of data visualisation, presenting information in a new and appealing way.

978075026918 — PLANET EARTH
9780750269056 — SPACE
9780750277822 — COUNTRIES
9780750269025 — MACHINES AND VEHICLES
9780750269063 — THE HUMAN BODY
9780750279642 — NATURAL RESOURCES
9780750269049 — THE HUMAN WORLD
9780750277815 — ANIMAL KINGDOM
9780750277792 — SPORT
9780750269032 — THE NATURAL WORLD
9780750279628 — ART AND ENTERTAINMENT
9780750277808 — TECHNOLOGY

Titles in the series

Planet Earth	Space	Countries
Machines and Vehicles	The Human Body	Natural Resources
The Human World	Animal Kingdom	Sport
The Natural World	Art and Entertainment	Technology